The AI Advantage for Small Businesses

Unlocking Growth, Efficiency, and Innovation with Smarter Tools

Written by
Eric LeBouthillier

AcraSolution | 2025 1st Edition
www.acrasolution.com

Preface

Why This Book Matters

Small businesses today face big challenges — tighter margins, growing competition, and rising customer expectations. Traditional strategies often fall short.

That's where AI steps in.

No longer reserved for tech giants, AI is now the most powerful, affordable tool small businesses can use to streamline operations, improve marketing, and scale faster.

But here's the problem: most SMBs don't know how to begin.

That's why this book exists.

The AI Advantage for Small Businesses is your practical guide — no jargon, no fluff. You'll learn how to:

- Use AI tools that save time and grow revenue
- Simplify your marketing and decision-making
- Compete smarter without needing a tech background

It's time to stop guessing and start using the tools that work.

Let's get started.

— Eric LeBouthillier
Author & Cybersecurity Strategist

LEGAL DISCLAIMER

Table of Contents

Who This Book Is For

This book is for small business owners, solopreneurs, and marketing professionals who want to grow smarter — not work harder.
You don't need to be a tech wizard or understand how algorithms work behind the scenes. You just need to know what tools to use, how to use them, and how to turn them into results. Whether you're managing your own marketing, building a business on the side, or trying to simplify your workflows, this guide is built to meet you where you are.
If you've ever said:

- "I don't have time to figure out AI."
- "I wish my marketing could run itself."
- "I want to grow, but not add more stress."

Then **this book was written for you.**
By the end, you'll know how to use AI to automate content, optimize ads, improve email performance, and make smarter decisions — without needing a big budget, a full team, or a technical background.

Chapter 1: Smarter, Not Harder: Why AI Is the New Competitive Edge

Introduction

Artificial Intelligence isn't some distant future or Silicon Valley-only phenomenon—it's here, now, and already transforming how smart businesses operate. And while large enterprises often grab headlines, it's actually small and midsize businesses (SMBs) that stand to gain the *most*. Why? Because AI levels the playing field. It gives lean teams superpowers, automates what used to be manual and expensive, and unlocks insights that once took full-time analysts to discover.

If you're running or managing an SMB, this chapter is your wake-up call. The AI revolution is no longer optional—it's your next competitive edge. In this chapter, we'll explore how the shift from manual work to machine-assisted thinking is reshaping industries, how SMBs are uniquely positioned to benefit, and what practical steps you can take today to future-proof your business while unlocking real ROI.

The AI Revolution Isn't Coming—It's Already Here

AI is no longer science fiction. It's behind the emails you receive, the ads you see, the support chats you use, and even the hiring tools many companies now rely on. What used to require a full IT department or data science team is now available at the click of a button or through a simple plug-in.

At its core, AI is about pattern recognition at scale. It takes massive amounts of data, finds meaningful patterns, and turns those into smart actions—whether that's predicting customer churn, automating bookkeeping, or detecting suspicious behavior in your cloud systems.

How this impacts SMBs:

- **Time Savings:** AI automates repetitive tasks like scheduling, invoicing, or lead follow-ups—giving your team back valuable hours.
- **Cost Reduction:** What used to take three staff members and 20 hours can now be done in five minutes with the right tool.
- **Smarter Decisions:** With AI, you don't need to "go with your gut"—you can go with real-time data and predictive insights.

Why SMBs Actually Have the Upper Hand

Big companies may have more data and bigger budgets—but they also have complex systems, rigid processes, and layers of decision-making. SMBs, on the other hand, can act quickly, pivot easily, and integrate AI solutions without years of red tape.

Here's why SMBs benefit more:

- **Agility:** You can adopt new AI tools in days—not months.
- **Fewer Dependencies:** Less legacy software to "undo" before bringing in automation.
- **Direct Impact:** Even a 10% time saving or 5% sales boost has a major impact on an SMB's bottom line.

Think of it like this: Big ships turn slowly. Small boats maneuver fast. And when you give those small boats a turbo engine—AI—they can outpace the giants.

Common SMB advantages with AI:

- Quicker implementation timelines
- Less internal resistance to change
- Lower costs to test and scale tools
- Closer connection to customer data and behavior

Mindset Shift: From Manual Labor to Machine-Assisted Thinking

For many SMB leaders, adopting AI isn't just about tools—it's about *mentality*. If you're used to doing things by hand, vetting every decision yourself, and trusting what's worked in the past, it can be uncomfortable to hand some of that over to automation.

But the truth is, AI doesn't replace your judgment—it *augments* it. Just like you use a calculator instead of doing long division, AI handles the heavy lifting so you can focus on strategy, relationships, and growth.

Key mindset shifts for SMB owners:

- From "I need to do everything myself" to "What can I offload safely?"
- From "That's too advanced for us" to "What's the *lightest lift* that gives us an edge?"
- From "We're not tech experts" to "We just need smart tools that do the work"

Tactical mindset shift tips:

- Start with one pain point (e.g., scheduling or customer emails)
- Try a no-code AI tool (covered in Chapter 2)
- Delegate outcomes, not just tasks (e.g., "find me the top 3 leads")

Real-World ROI: What AI Actually Delivers for SMBs

Let's break through the hype. What does AI *actually* do for SMBs when used correctly? Here's what business owners are already experiencing:

- **20% fewer customer service hours** through AI-powered chatbots
- **30% boost in email marketing ROI** with AI-generated content and timing
- **Faster hiring** with AI-assisted resume screening and interview scheduling
- **Reduced fraud and security issues** with AI threat detection tools

Case Study: The AI-Powered Accounting Firm

What happened:
A 12-person accounting firm in Ohio was spending over 25 hours a week on client reporting and month-end reconciliations. They started using an AI-powered bookkeeping assistant to automate data entry, categorize expenses, and generate draft reports.

What went right:
Within three months, they cut reporting time by 60%, repurposed staff to client advisory services, and grew their client base by 18%—without hiring anyone new.

What we learn:
Even highly skilled, traditional services like accounting can gain from machine-assisted workflows. The key was starting small—automating just one core process—and reinvesting time into high-value work.

Tactical AI Wins: What to Do Right Now

- Identify 1–2 repetitive or data-heavy tasks in your business
- Explore entry-level AI tools (more in Chapter 2)
- Shift from "what can I *do*" to "what can I *delegate* to software?"
- Talk to your team about where they lose time—these are your AI goldmines
- Start measuring time saved, not just cost saved

Common Pitfalls to Avoid:

- Waiting for a "perfect" tool—start with good enough
- Over-engineering: don't try to automate everything at once
- Ignoring your team's buy-in—people fear what they don't understand
- Not tracking results—make sure your AI use ties to time, money, or quality gains

---

The AI wave is here—and it's not just for tech giants. For SMBs, it's the great equalizer. It allows you to be faster, smarter, and more profitable without hiring a massive team or sinking huge dollars into infrastructure.

What's most exciting is that the tools are already available—and most don't require coding, training, or a technical background. The next chapter breaks down exactly how to start, what tools to explore, and how to tell if your business is ready.

Next Steps:
In **Chapter 2: Getting Started with AI: Tools, Terms & No-Code Tech**, we'll simplify the complex. You'll learn what AI really means, which tools to try first, and how to build your "AI starter kit"—even if you've never used AI before.

Chapter 2: Getting Started with AI: Tools, Terms & No-Code Tech

Introduction

By now, you understand that AI isn't just for Fortune 500 companies with deep pockets—it's for *you*. Whether you're running a small retail shop, a legal practice, a design agency, or a five-person tech firm, AI can give your team a major advantage without requiring you to become a programmer or hire expensive consultants.

This chapter is your gateway. We'll keep it simple, practical, and non-technical. You'll learn what AI actually means, how to talk about it with confidence, and which tools you can start using today—most of them free or low-cost. We'll also explore no-code platforms that let you build AI-powered automations in minutes and wrap up with an "AI-Ready" checklist to ensure your business is primed for the future.

Demystifying AI: What It Is (and Isn't)

Before diving into tools, we need to level-set. The biggest barrier to AI adoption in small businesses isn't cost—it's confusion. Many owners and managers still think AI means robots, complex algorithms, or needing a data science degree.

AI (Artificial Intelligence) refers to software that can learn from data, identify patterns, and make predictions or decisions—without being explicitly programmed for each scenario. It's not magic, it's math at scale.

Key related terms:

- **Machine Learning:** A subset of AI where systems improve over time by analyzing data.
- **Natural Language Processing (NLP):** The ability of AI to understand and generate human language.
- **Generative AI:** Tools that can create content—like text, images, or code—based on your input.
- **No-Code Platforms:** Tools that let non-developers build automations, apps, or AI workflows without writing a single line of code.

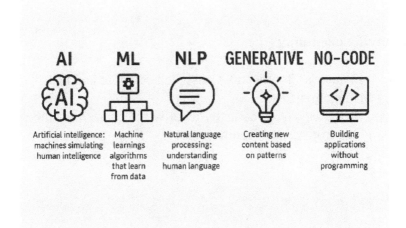

AI	ML	NLP	GENERATIVE	NO-CODE
Artificial intelligence: machines simulating human intelligence	Machine learnings algorithms that learn from data	Natural language processing: understanding human language	Creating new content based on patterns	Building applications without programming

The Best Free (or Affordable) AI Tools for SMBs

You don't need to spend thousands to start. Many of the most effective AI tools are either free to try or come with affordable business plans. The key is choosing the right tool for your specific need—not the flashiest one.

Here's a breakdown by function:

Content Creation

- **ChatGPT** (OpenAI): Generate blog ideas, marketing copy, email drafts, and customer responses.
- **Jasper**: AI writer built for teams and agencies, great for brand voice control.
- **Copy.ai**: Templates for landing pages, ads, and product descriptions.

Customer Support

- **Tidio** or **Zoho SalesIQ**: AI-powered live chat for websites, integrates with CRM.
- **HelpScout AI Assist**: Drafts replies for support tickets, reducing response time.

Admin & Scheduling

- **Motion** or **Clockwise**: AI-assisted calendar and task management.
- **Fireflies.ai**: Automatically records and transcribes meeting notes from Zoom, Teams, etc.

Data & Analytics

- **ChatGPT Advanced Data Analysis (formerly Code Interpreter)**: Helps interpret spreadsheets and financial data with plain language.
- **MonkeyLearn**: Text analysis for reviews, surveys, or support tickets.

Marketing & Automation

- **Zapier** with AI integrations: Connects your tools and automates repetitive tasks.
- **ManyChat**: Builds AI-powered chatbots for Facebook and Instagram.

Best Practices When Choosing AI Tools:

- Start with *one pain point* (content, support, scheduling, etc.)
- Pick tools with a free trial or freemium model
- Choose platforms with a strong user community or tutorials
- Avoid tools that require heavy setup or coding (unless you have internal support)

AI Tool	Free Trial	No-Code	Best For
Content	✓	✓	Blog Posts
Advertising	✓	✓	Ad Campaigns
Design	✓	✓	Marketing Visuals
Chatbots	✓	✓	Customer Support
	✓	✓	

No-Code = No Excuse

No-code platforms are a game-changer for SMBs. These tools let you build automated workflows, AI-powered chatbots, or even full applications—without writing code or hiring developers.

Top no-code solutions for small teams:

- **Zapier**: Automate "if-this-then-that" tasks across 6,000+ apps.
- **Airtable + ChatGPT**: Build interactive databases that generate content or answers.
- **Notion AI**: Your documents and task lists can now write themselves.
- **Bubble**: Build full web apps with AI-driven features (if you're ready to invest time).
- **Make (formerly Integromat)**: More complex automation for tech-savvy users.

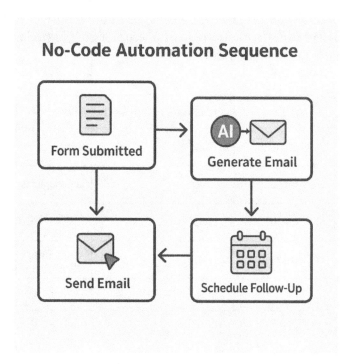

No-Code Automation Sequence

Use cases that take <30 minutes to set up:

- Auto-send a customer thank-you email after purchase
- Turn meeting notes into summaries and task lists
- Route leads from a form into your CRM and schedule follow-up
- Monitor competitor websites and summarize changes with AI

Checklist for choosing no-code tools:

- Drag-and-drop interface
- Free or low-cost tier
- Strong integration support (Zapier compatibility is a good sign)
- Templates or prebuilt workflows

The "AI-Ready" Checklist for Your Business

Not every SMB is ready to dive headfirst into AI, and that's okay. But a few small steps can dramatically increase your readiness—and your return.

The AI-Ready Checklist:

- ☑ We've identified 1–2 high-friction processes to automate
- ☑ We're using at least one no-code platform or AI-enhanced tool
- ☑ Our team understands the *why* behind trying AI tools
- ☑ We track metrics like time saved, response time, or lead quality
- ☑ We've assigned someone (or ourselves) to test new tools quarterly
- ☑ We're documenting what works, what fails, and what to repeat

Bonus Tip: Set a recurring 1-hour "AI Lab" session each month where your team tries out a new tool or explores a use case. It's low cost and often sparks surprising improvements.

Real-World Example: A Solo Realtor's AI Stack

What happened:
A solo real estate agent in British Columbia used to spend hours every week writing listing descriptions, responding to leads, and organizing appointments.

What they did:
They started using ChatGPT to write listing blurbs, Zapier to send leads from their site to a CRM and auto-reply with a booking link, and Fireflies.ai to take notes during showings.

What went right:

- Listing copy creation time dropped by 80%
- No leads went unacknowledged
- Time saved was reinvested into client outreach
- Revenue grew 22% in one quarter, without hiring anyone

What we learn:
Even solo operators can benefit hugely from a simple AI stack. The key was small, low-risk experiments that delivered visible gains fast.

Common Mistakes to Avoid

- **Trying too many tools at once:** You'll get overwhelmed and underwhelmed at the same time.
- **Not involving your team:** People support what they help create—let them explore and experiment.
- **Assuming free = worthless:** Some of the best AI breakthroughs happen on free-tier tools.
- **Skipping training or documentation:** Even "simple" tools work better with 30 minutes of learning.

Tactical Tips:

- Assign one person to test tools and share findings
- Use tool templates before building your own workflows
- Treat AI as a new team member—train it, test it, and trust it with time

AI is now as essential as email was in the early 2000s. You don't have to know how it works behind the scenes—you just need to know *what it can do for you*. And with today's no-code tools and free options, you can start with zero coding, minimal budget, and high upside.

Next Steps:
Now that you're AI-aware and equipped with beginner tools, we'll move into real-world application. In **Chapter 3: AI-Driven Content: Create Blogs, Emails & Social Posts in Minutes**, you'll learn how to use AI for marketing and communication—generating high-quality content in a fraction of the time, with clear workflows and powerful case studies.

Chapter 3: AI-Driven Content: Create Blogs, Emails & Social Posts in Minutes

Introduction

Content creation used to be one of the biggest time sinks for small businesses. Whether it was blog posts, newsletters, or social media updates, producing enough high-quality material to keep your brand visible often required hours of writing—or hiring expensive agencies. Not anymore.

With today's AI tools, content creation can take minutes, not days. And not just basic content—*on-brand, SEO-friendly, customer-relevant* material that actually drives engagement. This chapter will show you how to use AI to generate everything from blog articles to email campaigns and social posts. We'll unpack content workflows, repurposing tricks, and showcase real before-and-after examples from small teams who now do more with less.

The Rise of AI Content Creators

At the heart of this revolution are generative AI tools—software that can create human-sounding text from simple prompts. Tools like **ChatGPT**, **Jasper**, and **Copy.ai** are leading the charge, and the results are good enough to rival professional writers in many cases.

Here's what these tools can generate in seconds:

- Blog post drafts
- Catchy email subject lines
- Instagram captions
- Product descriptions
- LinkedIn updates
- YouTube video scripts
- SEO meta tags

What used to require a creative brief and a copywriter now takes a few clicks.

Top AI content tools for SMBs:

Tool	Best For	Price Point
ChatGPT	General-purpose writing & ideas	Free + Paid tiers
Jasper	Branded marketing content	$39+/mo
Copy.ai	Product copy, emails, social	Free + Pro options
Writesonic	Long-form SEO blog content	Affordable scaling

AI Content Tools

ChatGPT	Jasper
TOP USE CASES	**TOP USE CASES**
• Blog posts	• Blog posts
• Social media	• Social media
• Product descriptions	• Product descriptions

Blog Workflows with AI: From Idea to Publish

Blogging isn't dead—it's evolving. AI tools now help you brainstorm, outline, draft, and optimize posts with just a few guided prompts.

Step-by-step AI blog workflow:

1. **Brainstorm topics:**
   Use ChatGPT to generate titles based on your industry or keywords.
2. **Outline the structure:**
   Prompt your AI tool: "Create an outline for a 1,000-word blog post on [topic]."

3. **Generate content blocks:**
   Write each section individually using focused prompts to maintain clarity.
4. **Optimize for SEO:**
   Add keywords, rewrite intros, or create meta descriptions using tools like Surfer SEO or WriteSonic.
5. **Polish and fact-check:**
   Always edit manually to ensure brand voice accuracy and correctness.

Tips for better AI-written blogs:

- Provide examples, tone of voice, or structure in your prompt
- Break big tasks into chunks (don't ask for a full blog in one go)
- Use your own customer FAQs to feed ideas into the AI

Blog Content Pipeline

AI PROMPT   DRAFT

OPTIMIZE   PUBLISH

Email Automation Hacks Using AI

Email is still one of the highest ROI channels for SMBs. But writing regular newsletters, announcements, or campaign sequences is tedious. That's where AI jumps in.

What AI can generate in your email strategy:

- Subject lines with A/B test variations
- Personalized welcome emails
- Weekly newsletter summaries
- Re-engagement sequences
- Product launch campaigns

Sample Prompt:
"Write a warm, friendly email announcing a new seasonal menu for a local café. Include a 15% promo code."

Time-saving tactics:

- Use AI to turn blog posts into email digests
- Summarize webinars, podcasts, or videos into email-ready content
- Create variations for different audience segments with one click

AI-Generated Email

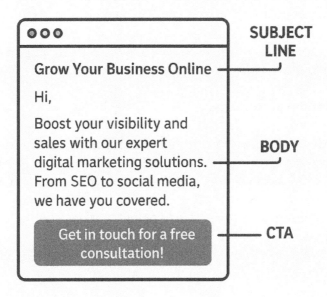

Grow Your Business Online — SUBJECT LINE

Hi,

Boost your visibility and sales with our expert digital marketing solutions. From SEO to social media, we have you covered. — BODY

Get in touch for a free consultation! — CTA

Repurposing Content Across Channels

One of the most powerful uses of AI is *content repurposing*—taking a single piece of content and spinning it into multiple formats and platforms.

Example: Turn one blog post into:

- A LinkedIn post summary
- A short Instagram caption
- A 3-step carousel on Canva
- A two-paragraph newsletter teaser
- A script for a short video or reel

Tools to help:

- **ChatGPT**: Rewrites content for different tones and lengths
- **Repurpose.io**: Converts video/audio clips into multiple formats
- **Descript**: Transcribes videos and turns them into blog content

Tactical repurposing tips:

- Always lead with your highest-performing content (top blog or email)
- Use AI to match tone to the platform (professional for LinkedIn, casual for IG)
- Batch-produce repurposed content weekly with the same input

Case Study: AI-Powered Content for a Local Fitness Studio

What happened:
A boutique fitness studio in Toronto needed to keep up with weekly blogs, newsletters, and Instagram posts—but had no dedicated marketing staff.

What they did:
They began using Copy.ai to generate weekly blog content and ChatGPT to repurpose it into email digests and social posts. Canva and Descript helped with visuals and short-form videos.

What went right:

- Time spent on content dropped from 10 hours/week to just 90 minutes
- Engagement on emails increased by 22%
- Instagram grew 40% in 4 months with more consistent, high-quality posting
- They launched a new class type using AI-generated customer surveys and content feedback

What we learn:
AI doesn't replace your creativity—it supercharges it. This studio took one blog per week and multiplied its impact across five different touchpoints.

Common Mistakes and Smart Fixes

Mistakes:

- Using AI content *as-is* without editing or fact-checking
- Relying too much on one tool (diversify your stack)
- Asking AI for vague tasks like "write a blog" without context
- Not aligning AI-generated content with your brand voice

Fixes:

- Create prompt templates your team can reuse
- Set aside 10–15 minutes to personalize and polish each piece
- Use tone-tuning tools (Jasper and ChatGPT both support style instructions)
- Build a "content calendar" that AI supports, not drives entirely

AI gives small businesses the power to produce high-quality content consistently, without hiring a full creative team. And when done right, it doesn't just save time—it increases reach, engagement, and conversions.

Next Steps:
You've seen how AI can accelerate your content engine. Now let's connect that content to your *sales and customer journey*. In **Chapter 4: Marketing Automation Made Easy: From Lead to Loyalty**, we'll explore how to build email sequences, test campaigns, and guide leads from first click to repeat purchase—on autopilot.

Chapter 4: Marketing Automation Made Easy: From Lead to Loyalty

Introduction

Marketing today isn't about blasting one message to everyone. It's about delivering the *right message* to the *right person* at the *right time*—and doing it without burning out your team. This is where marketing automation steps in, and thanks to AI, it's smarter and more accessible than ever for small businesses.

In this chapter, you'll learn how AI-powered automation helps you capture leads, guide them through the sales journey, and keep them engaged long after the sale. We'll break down the tools, techniques, and workflows that make this possible—from crafting email sequences and testing subject lines to behavioral segmentation and lead scoring. Whether you're nurturing first-time visitors or re-engaging cold leads, you'll see how automation turns missed opportunities into long-term loyalty.

Email Sequences That Work While You Sleep

An email sequence is a series of pre-written messages triggered by customer actions—like downloading a guide, abandoning a cart, or making a purchase. With the help of AI, these sequences can be dynamically adjusted, personalized, and optimized for better engagement.

Core types of email sequences:

- **Welcome series:** Introduce new subscribers to your brand and offers
- **Nurture series:** Educate and build trust with leads over time
- **Cart abandonment:** Recover lost sales with reminders and incentives
- **Post-purchase:** Increase retention, reviews, and upsells
- **Re-engagement:** Win back inactive subscribers with tailored offers

Best practices for building AI-assisted sequences:

- Use AI tools like **Sender AI** or **Mailchimp's Content Optimizer** to draft subject lines and content
- Personalize emails based on user behavior (browsing history, location, product interest)
- Use predictive send times to reach recipients when they're most likely to open

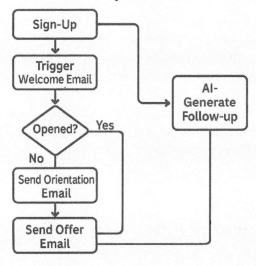

AI-Powered Welcome Email Sequence

Sign-Up → Trigger Welcome Email → Opened? — Yes → AI-Generate Follow-up; No → Send Orientation Email → Send Offer Email

A/B Testing Made Simple: Let AI Optimize for You

Testing subject lines, layouts, calls-to-action, or send times is one of the best ways to improve campaign performance. The problem? It's often skipped due to time constraints.

AI changes that by automating both test setup and analysis.

Key elements to A/B test:

- Subject lines (length, tone, urgency)
- Button text and placement
- Image vs. no image
- Personalization tags (name, location, product)

Tools that automate A/B testing:

- **Moosend** and **Mailchimp AI** automatically test and send winning variants
- **Brevo (formerly Sendinblue)** uses AI to recommend best-performing templates
- AI-generated content (from Jasper or ChatGPT) lets you quickly create multiple test versions

Quick tip: Always test one element at a time for clear insights, and run tests until you hit statistically meaningful sample sizes (your platform will help with this).

Behavioral Segmentation: Target Smarter, Not Harder

Generic marketing is dead. Segmentation allows you to tailor messages to different user behaviors—making your emails more relevant and more likely to convert.

Behavioral segmentation examples:

- Visitors who viewed pricing pages but didn't convert
- Past customers who haven't purchased in 90 days
- Leads who clicked on a specific blog post
- Subscribers who opened 3+ emails in a row (hot leads)

How AI improves segmentation:

- Predicts which leads are most likely to convert
- Clusters users based on behavior patterns
- Scores leads automatically based on engagement

Tools like **Sender, Ortto**, and **ActiveCampaign** let you trigger actions based on real-time data, not just static tags.

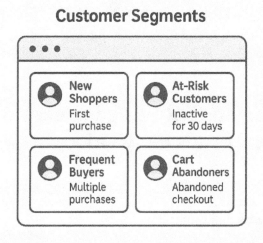

AI Tools to Power Your Marketing Automation

You don't need an enterprise budget to run powerful automation. These tools are designed for SMBs and come with AI baked in.

Tool	Strengths	Price Range
Mailchimp AI	Subject line suggestions, smart timing	Free–$60/month
Sender	Drag-and-drop automation builder	Free–$40/month
Moosend	AI-powered segmentation & analytics	Affordable plans
ActiveCampaign	Predictive sending + CRM integration	Mid-range plans

Features to look for:

- Visual workflow builders (easy drag-and-drop)
- Smart segmentation and tagging
- AI content or timing optimization
- Built-in analytics and A/B testing

Lead Scoring & Re-Engagement: Don't Let Warm Leads Go Cold

Not all leads are created equal. Lead scoring helps you prioritize who to follow up with—and AI makes it more accurate by analyzing behavior patterns you might miss.

Lead scoring factors AI can assess:

- Frequency of email opens
- Time spent on your website
- Engagement with specific products
- Social media interactions

Once leads are scored, you can segment them into:

- **Hot leads:** Route to sales or send high-converting offers
- **Warm leads:** Continue nurturing with valuable content
- **Cold leads:** Enroll in re-engagement sequences or sunset

Re-engagement tactics:

- Use AI to personalize subject lines with urgency or emotion
- Offer limited-time discounts or exclusive content
- Create "We Miss You" sequences with exit surveys

Email Campaign Performance

	Traditional	AI-Optimized
Open Rate		▬▬▬
Click Rate		▬▬
Conver-sions		▬▬▬

Real-World Example: Automated Growth for an Online Course Creator

What happened:
A solo business coach selling an online course was manually emailing prospects and struggling to keep up with nurturing and follow-ups.

What they did:
They implemented Mailchimp's AI-powered automation to send welcome sequences, auto-tag leads by interest level, and re-engage inactive users with special offers.

What went right:

- Time spent on email dropped by 80%
- Sales grew by 35% in three months
- Re-engagement emails brought back over 120 dormant leads
- Lead scoring allowed them to prioritize high-intent users for personalized outreach

What we learn:
Even a solo operator can use automation to act like a full marketing team. The key was letting AI handle the timing, targeting, and testing—while the owner focused on refining the offer.

Common Mistakes to Avoid

Don't:

- Use one-size-fits-all email content
- Neglect to test subject lines or timing
- Assume leads will remember you without regular contact
- Let re-engagement sequences feel like spam

Do:

- Set up a basic lead scoring system, even if it's simple
- Monitor open and click-through rates monthly
- Use AI for content *ideas*, but always review for tone
- Keep your automations updated as offers or products change

Marketing automation isn't just a time-saver—it's a growth engine. When paired with AI, it becomes smarter, faster, and more personal. For small businesses, this means higher ROI, more consistent outreach, and customers who stay connected from first touch to loyal fan.

Next Steps:
Now that your email marketing is optimized and automated, let's take that same intelligence and apply it to your advertising. In **Chapter 5: Ad Campaigns That Learn: Smarter Facebook, Google, and LinkedIn Ads**, we'll explore how AI takes the guesswork out of paid campaigns, helping you reach the right people, spend less, and earn more.

Chapter 5: Ad Campaigns That Learn: Smarter Facebook, Google, and LinkedIn Ads

Introduction

Running ads used to be like throwing darts blindfolded. You'd choose a budget, pick some keywords, write an ad, and hope for the best. Fast forward to today, and AI has completely flipped the script. Modern ad platforms now *learn* from every click, scroll, and purchase—automatically adjusting your campaigns to boost performance and lower costs.

In this chapter, we'll unpack how AI has transformed online advertising. You'll learn how to use AI-driven tools on platforms like Facebook (Meta), Google, and LinkedIn to bid smarter, target better, and run dynamic, personalized ads. Plus, we'll cover real strategies for small businesses to cut waste and boost ROI—no agency needed.

AI-Powered Targeting and Bidding

Every major ad platform now uses AI to automate the most complex parts of campaign management—like who to target, when to show your ad, and how much to bid.

Here's what AI handles for you:

- **Real-time bidding:** Adjusts bids based on likelihood of conversion
- **Audience targeting:** Learns which users engage most with your offer
- **Ad placement optimization:** Puts your ad in the best possible spot across networks
- **Budget efficiency:** Maximizes your spend across multiple ad sets

How this helps SMBs:

- No need to manually adjust bids every day
- Reduces wasted spend on underperforming audiences
- Improves ad performance over time without constant tweaking

HOW AI BIDDING WORKS

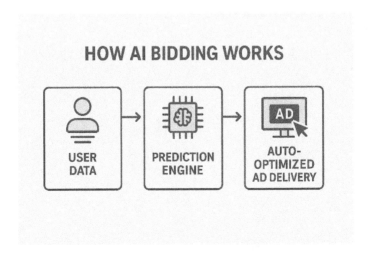

USER DATA → PREDICTION ENGINE → AUTO-OPTIMIZED AD DELIVERY

Dynamic Ad Variations: One Input, Many Outputs

Gone are the days of writing one static ad. With dynamic ad tools, you can feed in several headlines, descriptions, and images—then let AI mix and match combinations to find the best performer.

Platforms that support dynamic content:

- **Facebook (Meta Advantage+):** Automatically tests headlines, CTAs, and visuals
- **Google Ads (Responsive Search + Display):** AI creates multiple versions from a content pool
- **LinkedIn Campaign Manager:** Uses multiple versions to optimize professional messaging

Tactical tips for dynamic ads:

- Input at least 3–5 headline and text variations
- Use diverse imagery to see what drives clicks
- Let campaigns run for a full week before evaluating results
- Use AI-generated copy as a creative springboard

Prompt idea for ad writing:
"Write 3 headline variations and 3 description lines for a local cleaning service targeting homeowners. Tone: friendly and professional."

Lookalike Audiences and Geo-Targeting Made Smarter

AI isn't just great at finding *your* audience—it's great at finding *others just like them*. With lookalike modeling, ad platforms analyze your current customers and find similar users based on behavior, interests, and demographics.

Key uses of AI-enhanced audience targeting:

- **Lookalike audiences:** Reach people who resemble your best customers
- **Custom audiences:** Retarget website visitors or email list subscribers
- **Geo-targeting:** Show ads only to people within a defined radius or region

Example strategies:

- Target past purchasers with upsell offers
- Use geo-targeted ads for local event promotions
- Build lookalikes from your top 1% of spenders

Smart move: Combine AI targeting with AI creative. You'll let the system optimize *who sees what*—and that's when costs drop and conversion rates climb.

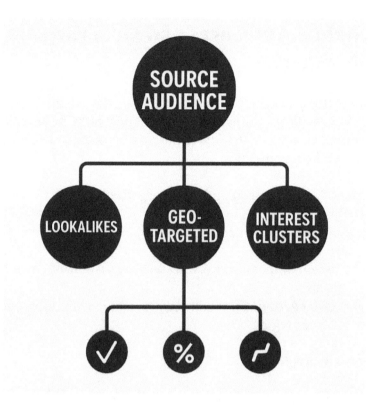

Tools That Do the Heavy Lifting

You don't need to master every detail of ad management. These tools use AI to make launching, managing, and optimizing campaigns a breeze—even for solo founders or small teams.

Top AI ad tools for SMBs:

Tool	Platform	What It Does
Meta Advantage+	Facebook/Instagram	Auto-optimizes creative and placement
Performance Max	Google Ads	Manages search, display, video in one campaign

Tool	Platform	What It Does
AdCreative.ai	Cross-platform	Generates high-converting ad designs & copy
Smartly.io	Facebook & TikTok	Automated creative + A/B testing tools
Revealbot	Cross-platform	Automates campaign scaling and reporting

Checklist for tool selection:

- Choose a platform-native tool first (e.g., Meta Advantage+)
- Start with a single objective (leads, traffic, or conversions)
- Avoid over-automation—monitor performance weekly
- Combine automation with strong creative input

Case Study: How a Local Furniture Brand Slashed Ad Costs with AI

What happened:
A small furniture store in Denver was spending $2,000/month on Facebook and Google Ads, manually managing every campaign with little return.

What they did:
They switched to Meta Advantage+ and Google's Performance Max campaigns. They used dynamic creative, uploaded past purchaser lists for lookalike modeling, and fed in AI-generated headlines and descriptions from AdCreative.ai.

What went right:

- CPC dropped 41% within 6 weeks
- Conversion rate increased by 28%
- ROI on ad spend more than doubled
- Time spent managing ads dropped from 6 hours/week to under 1

What we learn:
AI-driven ad campaigns remove much of the guesswork. With the right creative input and a few smart automation settings, even modest ad budgets go further.

BEFORE | AFTER

MANUAL CAMPAIGN	AI-OPTIMIZED CAMPAIGN
CPC $0.80	CPC $0.40
CONVERSIONS 100	CONVERSIONS 250

Common Mistakes (and How to Avoid Them)

Mistakes:

- Letting AI run ads without monitoring performance
- Not testing enough creative variations
- Targeting too broad or too narrow an audience
- Ignoring post-click experience (landing page matters too!)

Fixes:

- Set clear goals for each campaign (traffic, leads, sales)
- Monitor weekly, adjust monthly
- Use both AI-generated and human-refined ad copy
- Align ad promise with landing page messaging

AI has turned advertising into a learning machine—literally. Instead of guessing what works, platforms now *test and learn* in real time. For SMBs, this means you can compete with much bigger players and get more from every dollar you spend.

Next Steps:
You've launched smart ads and brought in traffic—now it's time to convert. In **Chapter 6: Building Funnels with AI: From First Click to Final Sale**, we'll guide you through creating landing pages, mapping your funnel journey, and turning AI-powered insights into real sales.

Chapter 6: Building Funnels with AI: From First Click to Final Sale

Introduction

Getting traffic to your website is just step one. Converting that traffic into leads, customers, and repeat buyers—that's where the real challenge (and opportunity) lies. Enter the **AI-powered funnel**: a streamlined, automated journey that takes visitors from curiosity to conversion using smart landing pages, personalized content, and behavior-driven follow-ups.

In this chapter, you'll learn how to build a high-converting sales funnel using AI tools without needing a dev team or agency. From landing page optimization and lead scoring to automation sequences and real-world SMB examples, you'll see exactly how modern funnels are built—and how to let AI do the heavy lifting.

Optimizing Landing Pages with AI Tools

Your funnel starts with a landing page. Whether you're promoting a product, collecting emails, or offering a free resource, that page needs to load fast, look great, and convert.

Top AI-enhanced landing page platforms:

- **Unbounce Smart Builder**: Uses AI to create layouts and suggest copy based on your goals.
- **Instapage**: Offers heatmaps and A/B testing powered by machine learning.
- **Landingi**: Simplified builder with templates that adapt to your audience segments.

AI can assist with:

- Generating persuasive headlines
- Suggesting CTAs based on audience behavior
- Personalizing page content by visitor source (e.g., email vs. ad)

Pro tip: Ask ChatGPT to generate headline variations based on different buyer personas or traffic sources.

Mapping the Funnel Journey

Think of your funnel as a guided experience—from first touch to final sale. AI makes it easier to track, analyze, and refine each stage based on real-time data.

Key funnel stages:

1. **Attract:** Ads, social, SEO bring traffic
2. **Capture:** Landing page collects contact info
3. **Nurture:** Automated emails & content build trust
4. **Convert:** Offers and CTAs trigger purchase
5. **Retain:** Post-sale emails, support, upsells

AI can enhance:

- Predicting drop-off points in the funnel
- Optimizing email send timing and content
- Identifying the most common paths to purchase

Tools like Funnels.ai and **Ortto** help visualize these journeys and flag bottlenecks automatically.

Lead Scoring with AI: Prioritize the Right Prospects

Not all leads are created equal. AI lead scoring helps you identify who's ready to buy—and who needs more nurturing.

How it works:

- Assigns scores to leads based on actions (e.g., clicks, downloads, time on site)
- Prioritizes follow-ups for high-intent leads
- Integrates with CRMs and email tools to adjust messaging automatically

Tools that offer AI lead scoring:

- **HubSpot AI**
- **Freshsales**
- **Zoho CRM Plus**

Example:
A lead who views your pricing page twice and downloads a brochure might score 80/100. One who reads a blog but never clicks anything scores 20/100.

AI LEAD SCORING

BEHAVIOR	0	25	50	75
Downloaded eBook				
Submitted Contact Form				
Opened Email				
Visited Pricing Page				

LEAD SCORE

Triggered Automation Sequences That Convert

Once you've scored a lead, automation takes over. Using triggers and workflows, AI tools deliver the right message at the right time—without lifting a finger.

Automation examples:

- Lead visits pricing page → send case study email
- Downloads a guide → start 3-email nurture series
- Abandons cart → trigger discount offer + follow-up
- Opens 3+ emails → route to sales team

Tools that support AI-triggered workflows:

- **ActiveCampaign**
- **Keap (formerly Infusionsoft)**
- **Ortto**
- **Mailchimp Journey Builder**

Best practices:

- Start with one trigger and build from there
- Keep sequences short and focused (2–4 emails max)
- Use personalization—include name, behavior references, or product viewed

---

Real SMB Success Story: Coaching Funnel That Runs Itself

Who:
A life coach running a solo consulting practice in Austin

The challenge:
She was spending too much time manually following up with leads from webinars and discovery calls—and losing hot prospects in the shuffle.

What she did:

- Built a landing page with **Unbounce Smart Builder**
- Connected it to a funnel mapped in **ActiveCampaign**
- Used AI to score leads and segment them into nurture or sales-ready lists
- Triggered email sequences based on page views and form completions

The results:

- Increased lead-to-client conversion rate by **39%**
- Cut admin time by **8+ hours/week**
- Her calendar now auto-books based on lead scoring triggers
- She added a group coaching tier thanks to the time saved

Lesson:
You don't need a big team to run a smart funnel—just the right stack and a clear strategy.

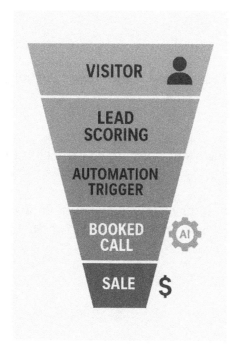

Common Funnel Mistakes and Fixes

Mistakes:

- Sending all leads the same content
- Relying on guesswork instead of data
- Forgetting post-sale engagement
- Not aligning funnel with your actual buyer journey

Fixes:

- Use AI to map and adjust journey stages
- Segment leads early and personalize content
- Include post-purchase sequences to increase retention
- Review funnel performance monthly (bounce rate, open rate, conversion rate)

A modern funnel is more than a form and a thank-you page—it's a living, learning system powered by data. With AI, you can stop guessing and start guiding each visitor through a smart, responsive journey that adapts in real time. And when done right, it doesn't just boost sales—it frees your time.

Next Steps:
Now that your funnel is working behind the scenes, let's focus on what happens *on* the scene—your website. In **Chapter 7: Website Intelligence: Personalization and Predictive Offers**, we'll explore how AI tailors your website to each visitor, increasing time on page, engagement, and conversions with every click.

Chapter 7: Website Intelligence: Personalization and Predictive Offers

Introduction

Your website isn't just a digital brochure—it's your most valuable 24/7 salesperson. But if it treats every visitor the same, it's missing huge opportunities. Today's leading websites don't just display information—they *react*, *adapt*, and *predict*. With AI-powered personalization, even small business websites can feel like they were custom-built for each visitor.

In this chapter, we'll explore how to turn your website into an intelligent, behavior-aware experience. From dynamic content and chatbots to personalized offers and smart pop-ups, you'll see how AI helps your site engage more users, reduce bounce, and convert better—automatically.

AI-Driven User Experiences: Why One-Size No Longer Fits All

Today's visitors expect your website to understand their needs—even before they tell you. AI enables that by analyzing behavior in real time and adapting the content or layout accordingly.

Here's how AI personalizes the experience:

- Recognizes if someone is a returning visitor or first-timer
- Adapts homepage messages based on referral source (e.g., email vs. ad)
- Shows different CTAs depending on user behavior (browsing vs. buying)
- Recommends products based on browsing or purchase history

Real impacts for SMBs:

- Lower bounce rates
- Higher time on site
- Increased lead form submissions
- Better conversion on product or service pages

Pro Tip: Use AI tools to dynamically update your homepage, offer banners, or testimonials based on the visitor's segment.

STATIC WEBSITE

CALL TO ACTION

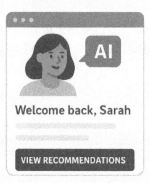

PERSONALIZED WEBSITE

AI

Welcome back, Sarah

VIEW RECOMMENDATIONS

Dynamic Content Based on Behavior

AI watches and learns how visitors interact with your site—then serves up content that matches their intent.

Common dynamic personalization tactics:

- **Content swap:** Change headlines or sections based on location, source, or user type
- **Progressive forms:** Shorten or expand forms depending on known user data
- **Exit-intent popups:** Trigger offers or surveys just before a user bounces
- **Smart banners:** Adjust offers based on browsing patterns

Tools that power dynamic content:

- **RightMessage:** Tailors site messaging to visitor segments
- **Optimizely AI:** Tests and adapts layouts and headlines in real-time
- **Tidio:** Combines chatbot logic with personalized pop-ups

Example workflow:
Visitor clicks on a Facebook ad → visits your pricing page → sees a popup offering a 10% discount valid for 20 minutes → returns two days later and sees a "schedule a demo" banner instead.

Conversational Touchpoints: Chatbots, Pop-Ups, Exit Offers

Conversational AI gives your visitors a way to interact *before* they fill out a form or make a decision—resulting in more leads and fewer bounces.

Key tools:

- **Tidio**: Combines chatbot, pop-up, and live chat in one platform
- **Drift**: B2B chatbot that qualifies leads automatically
- **HubSpot Chatflows**: Free chatbot builder with CRM integration

Top use cases:

- Lead capture via short conversation
- Product recommendations
- Booking a consultation
- Collecting feedback or survey responses

Best practices:

- Start with one goal (e.g., schedule calls, answer FAQs)
- Keep chatbot flows short and friendly
- Include an option to talk to a human when needed

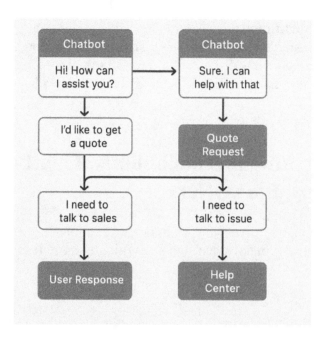

Tools That Make Your Website Smarter

You don't need a developer to deploy intelligent personalization. These tools offer intuitive dashboards, smart triggers, and AI-powered recommendations for small business websites.

Top AI website intelligence tools:

Tool	Key Features	Best For
HubSpot AI	CRM data + website personalization	Service & sales sites
Tidio	Chatbots, popups, behavior tracking	Retail & appointment
RightMessage	Personalized CTAs and content by segment	Email-driven sites
OptiMonk	Smart pop-ups and product recommender AI	E-commerce

Checklist to start:

- ✅ Install one behavior-aware chatbot or popup tool
- ✅ Identify 1–2 high-traffic pages to personalize
- ✅ Start A/B testing CTAs by segment
- ✅ Use Google Analytics to track performance before and after

---

Real-World Example: Personalized Offers That Converted 3X Better

Business type:
A boutique travel agency offering custom vacation packages

Challenge:
Website had high traffic but very low form completion. Most visitors browsed and left without interaction.

What they did:

- Installed **RightMessage** to detect visitor source (e.g., organic search vs. paid ad)
- Tailored homepage headline and CTA to match interests: "Luxury Italy Getaway" vs. "Budget Family Trips"
- Used **Tidio** to launch a chatbot asking: "Where would you love to go next?" with quick answer buttons
- Added exit popup with a free downloadable guide, triggered by cursor movement

Results after 60 days:

- Form submissions increased by **312%**
- Time on site jumped by **41%**
- Bounce rate dropped by **26%**
- 17 new leads converted into booked consultations—without increasing ad spend

Lesson:
Small changes—when powered by smart tools—can lead to massive improvements in performance.

Mistakes to Avoid with AI Website Tools

Mistakes:

- Personalizing too much, too soon—leading to confusion or errors
- Overusing popups or chatbots that annoy rather than assist
- Not connecting your tools to your CRM or email list
- Forgetting to test against a control group (A/B testing is key)

Fixes:

- Start small: personalize one section or CTA
- Monitor visitor engagement weekly
- Integrate your tools to sync data and follow-ups
- Use tools with built-in analytics to optimize performance

AI doesn't just make your website prettier—it makes it *smarter*. It listens, learns, and responds to your visitors, helping them find what they need faster while nudging them toward action. The result? More leads, happier customers, and a better experience for everyone.

Next Steps:
Your website is now a smart conversion engine. But how do you measure its impact and improve even further? In **Chapter 8: Analytics That Actually Matter: Metrics, Predictions, and Clarity**, we'll break down the AI-powered dashboards and predictive insights that help you make data-driven decisions—not just reports.

Chapter 8: Analytics That Actually Matter: Metrics, Predictions, and Clarity

Introduction

Let's be honest—most analytics dashboards are cluttered, confusing, and rarely lead to action. For small businesses, the goal isn't to collect *more* data; it's to get *smarter* with the data you already have. That's where AI-powered analytics shine. Instead of static reports, you get living insights—metrics that learn, alert you to trends, and even recommend what to do next.

This chapter focuses on the analytics that actually move the needle. From user behavior predictions and churn alerts to AI dashboards that do the thinking for you, we'll break down how to stop drowning in data and start driving decisions.

AI Dashboards: Smarter Insights Without the Noise

Forget staring at 50 charts trying to figure out what changed last week. AI-enhanced dashboards cut through the noise and bring forward the trends and anomalies that actually matter.

Top AI analytics platforms for SMBs:

- **Google Analytics 4 (GA4):** Event-based tracking + predictive metrics (free)
- **Piwik PRO:** GDPR-compliant alternative with strong AI integrations
- **Looker Studio (Google):** Custom dashboards that visualize complex data clearly
- **Zoho Analytics:** Easy AI-powered reports with natural language queries

How AI improves your dashboards:

- Highlights user drop-off points and funnel leaks
- Predicts which users are likely to convert or churn
- Recommends next actions (e.g., "optimize mobile load time")

Pro tip: Use GA4's "predictive audiences" to target users most likely to purchase in the next 7 days.

Predictive Analytics: See What's Coming Before It Happens

Rather than just analyzing what *already* happened, predictive analytics uses AI to forecast what's *likely* to happen next. This allows SMBs to be proactive—adjusting campaigns, offers, or support in real time.

Examples of predictive use cases:

- Forecasting next week's sales based on current trends
- Identifying which customers are likely to buy again
- Anticipating seasonal slowdowns in traffic
- Estimating email campaign performance before launch

Tools that offer built-in predictive features:

- **Zoho CRM Plus**
- **Piwik PRO Predictive Suite**
- **HubSpot's Predictive Lead Scoring**
- **Ortto's Customer Journey Predictions**

How to start:

- Choose one area: leads, churn, or sales
- Use your existing data (visits, form fills, purchases)
- Run small tests to see if predictions hold up—then scale

Churn Detection: Save Customers Before They Leave

It costs 5x more to acquire a new customer than to keep an existing one—yet most SMBs don't spot churn signals until it's too late. AI helps you detect early warning signs and act before the relationship is lost.

Churn signals AI tools watch for:

- Decreased site visits or email opens
- Longer response time between actions
- Decline in average order size
- Negative survey or chatbot sentiment

Smart actions triggered by churn alerts:

- Send a re-engagement offer or bonus
- Offer a personal check-in or feedback form
- Change email frequency or content style

Tools that assist:

- **Baremetrics** (for SaaS and subscriptions)
- **HubSpot Service Hub**
- **Custify** (automated churn scoring and alerts)

From Reporting to Real Decisions: What to Track and Why

It's easy to fall into the trap of tracking *everything*—page views, bounce rate, likes, click-throughs—without tying any of it to real business outcomes.

Let's simplify it.

Track these if you want growth:

- **Conversion Rate:** % of users who take your intended action (e.g., sign up, buy, book)
- **Customer Lifetime Value (CLV):** How much a customer is worth over time
- **Churn Rate:** % of customers who don't come back or cancel
- **Attribution Paths:** How people *actually* find and convert on your site

AI can help by:

- Visualizing journey maps to show high-converting paths
- Grouping users by behavioral patterns
- Suggesting actions based on performance shifts

Example:
If conversions dip and mobile traffic is up, AI might flag "check mobile load speed" as a possible fix.

Real-World Example: Making Decisions That Grew Revenue 22%

Who:
A regional subscription-based meal delivery service

Challenge:
They had solid traffic and growing email lists—but couldn't figure out why their churn rate kept creeping up.

What they did:

- Switched from basic Google Analytics to GA4 and Zoho Analytics
- Used predictive churn scoring to identify at-risk customers
- Ran a survey via chatbot to collect quick feedback from those users
- Offered personalized coupon codes + recipe previews as incentives to stay

Results:

- Reduced monthly churn by 19%
- Added $18K in retained revenue in 90 days
- Implemented weekly decision reviews using only AI dashboard highlights

Lesson:
They didn't need more data—they needed *actionable* data. And that came from smart dashboards and simplified tracking.

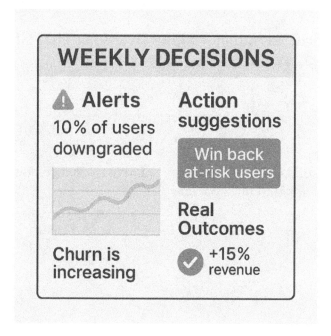

Common Mistakes and How to Fix Them

Mistakes:

- Relying on default dashboards without context
- Tracking vanity metrics with no tie to revenue
- Ignoring churn signals until it's too late
- Reporting without acting on insights

Fixes:

- Build a "North Star" metric dashboard tied to growth
- Set thresholds for alerts (e.g., >30% drop triggers review)
- Ask your dashboard, "What should we do next?"—not just "What happened?"
- Schedule monthly data-action meetings—even if it's just you

---

With the right setup, your analytics don't just tell you *what* happened—they show you *what's next*. That shift is the difference between playing catch-up and staying one step ahead. For SMBs, AI-powered analytics turn confusion into clarity and hesitation into confident action.

Next Steps:
Now that you know how to track what matters, it's time to talk about *how you use AI responsibly*. In **Chapter 9: Cyber-Aware Marketing: Ethics, Transparency, and Trust with AI**, we'll explore the ethical and legal side of AI—from disclosure and bias to trust-building and protection.

Chapter 9: Cyber-Aware Marketing: Ethics, Transparency, and Trust with AI

Introduction

AI can do amazing things—but just because it *can* doesn't mean it *should*. As businesses adopt more automation and personalization, consumers are asking tougher questions: "Am I being tracked?" "Is this decision biased?" "Is this experience authentic—or artificial?"

Trust is the currency of modern marketing. And in a world where AI can create, predict, and persuade, your *ethical choices* set you apart.

In this chapter, we'll unpack how to use AI in marketing *responsibly*—without crossing into creepy, biased, or misleading territory. You'll learn how to disclose AI use appropriately, reduce ethical risk without needing complex legal reviews, and implement an "Ethical AI Checklist" designed for real-world SMBs.

Avoiding Bias, Over-Personalization, and Creepy UX

AI learns from patterns—but those patterns aren't always fair. If you're not careful, you can unintentionally exclude customers, reinforce stereotypes, or make people feel watched instead of welcomed.

Common ethical traps:

- **Bias in training data:** If your AI learns from past behaviors, it may carry forward unintentional prejudice (e.g., targeting only one demographic).
- **Over-personalization:** Showing someone a product they *just* talked about offline may feel invasive.
- **Predictive creep:** Offering discounts based on assumed income level or family status without consent.

Real-world red flags:

- A user visits once and suddenly sees 5 retargeting ads everywhere they go
- Your chatbot "knows" the person's name before they typed anything
- Ads or popups seem to know private data the customer never gave you

Guiding principle: Personalization should *feel helpful*, not like surveillance.

How to Disclose AI Use Properly

People don't mind that AI is involved—they mind when it's hidden. Studies show that transparency *increases* trust and engagement, especially with things like content, recommendations, or chatbot interactions.

When to disclose AI use:

- When AI is writing or suggesting content (e.g., email copy, blog post summaries)
- When chatbots handle support or lead qualification
- When offers or pricing are personalized algorithmically

Simple ways to disclose:

- "This email was co-written with smart AI tools"
- "You're chatting with our virtual assistant, powered by AI"
- "These recommendations are generated based on your browsing preferences"

Do NOT:
Use AI to simulate a human advisor without disclosure—it's misleading and, in some cases, legally risky.

Data Responsibility Without Data Hoarding

You don't need to collect every piece of data to be smart. In fact, storing too much data increases your liability. Modern AI tools allow *zero-data personalization*—where no personal info is stored, yet experiences are still tailored.

Smarter, safer practices:

- Use session-based personalization (real-time, no storage)
- Anonymize data whenever possible
- Avoid collecting data you don't *actively use*
- Delete inactive user data on a schedule

Tools that help you stay compliant:

- **Piwik PRO** (GDPR-friendly analytics with full user control)
- **Didomi** and **Osano** (cookie consent & data compliance automation)
- **RightMessage** (personalization without storing identifiable info)

Best practice: Include a clear, plain-language privacy statement on your site. Let users opt out of personalized features if they want to.

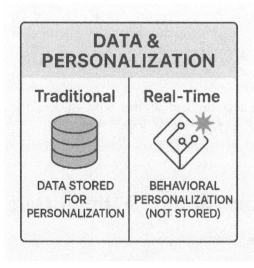

Tools That Protect Without Complexity

You don't need a legal department to stay ethical. Many AI marketing platforms now include built-in safeguards and privacy-first settings that keep your business on the right side of the line.

Top tools with ethics-first features:

Tool	Ethical Feature	Best For
HubSpot AI	Consent-based lead scoring & chatflows	B2B service businesses
Tidio	Clear chatbot disclosures + privacy flags	SMBs & eCommerce
RightMessage	Anonymous user segmentation	Content marketing funnels
Osano	Global privacy compliance toolkit	Sites with global traffic

Checklist to evaluate your tools:

- ☑ Does it collect only what's necessary?
- ☑ Is AI involvement disclosed to the user?
- ☑ Can users opt out of personalization or tracking?
- ☑ Are privacy settings easy to configure (not buried)?
- ☑ Is data encrypted and auto-purged when no longer needed?

Your "Ethical AI Checklist" for Marketing

Use this as your internal guide before launching any AI-powered campaign:

Ethical AI Checklist for SMBs:

- ☑ Have we disclosed AI involvement clearly and honestly?
- ☑ Could this personalization feel invasive or unfair?
- ☑ Is our data use limited, respectful, and compliant?
- ☑ Have we tested outputs for bias (e.g., gender, location)?
- ☑ Are there human fail-safes or override options in place?
- ☑ Do our tools default to privacy—not just performance?

Bonus Tip: Ask your team or customers—*"Would this creep you out?"* If the answer's yes, dial it back.

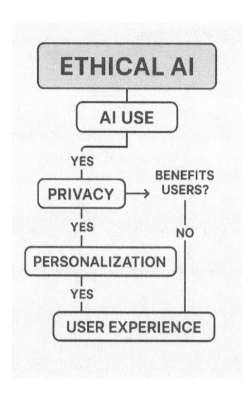

Real-World Example: Building Trust Through Transparency

Business type:
A small HR tech startup offering a job-matching platform

Challenge:
They used AI to suggest candidate-employer matches—but early users felt uncomfortable not knowing how the system worked.

What they did:

- Added a "How this works" section explaining their AI logic in plain terms
- Gave users control to refine or override their AI matches

- Displayed a badge: "AI-Recommended Based on Your Profile + Preferences"
- Stopped showing salary-prediction data unless users requested it

Results:

- User satisfaction jumped by 24%
- Churn dropped significantly for new trial accounts
- They were praised on LinkedIn for "setting a new transparency standard"
- 3 enterprise clients signed on after the policy update

Lesson:
Transparency doesn't slow you down—it strengthens your brand. People trust what they understand and *feel in control of.*

Mistakes to Avoid with Ethical AI in Marketing

Mistakes:

- Letting AI run unchecked without oversight
- Copy-pasting human names or personas over bots
- Gathering more user data "just in case"
- Ignoring regional privacy laws or platform policies

Fixes:

- Review your AI tools' privacy settings quarterly
- Label all chatbot and AI-generated content
- Use data-minimization defaults (only store what's useful)
- Stay updated on legal standards (especially GDPR, CCPA, and platform-specific terms)

Ethical AI marketing is about being honest, respectful, and user-first. It doesn't require perfection—it requires *intention*. For small businesses, doing the right thing isn't just moral—it's strategic. The brands that win trust now will earn loyalty long after the buzzwords fade.

Next Steps:
In our final chapter, we'll zoom out and look at the full system. **Chapter 10: The AI Marketing Engine: How to Scale, Systemize & Sell More** will show you how to bring everything together into a repeatable, streamlined machine—ready to grow with your business.

Chapter 10: The AI Marketing Engine: How to Scale, Systemize & Sell More

Introduction

You've explored the tools, mastered the workflows, and seen the results. Now it's time to scale. This chapter brings everything together—content, automation, analytics, ethics—into a unified *AI-powered marketing engine*. For SMBs, this means growing smarter without growing overhead, and expanding reach without losing control.

We'll cover how to automate your backend, when to outsource vs. automate, and how to build a scalable system that runs with minimal effort. Plus, you'll get a 5-year roadmap to help your team evolve as AI tools continue to grow.

Bringing It All Together: The Full AI Stack

Throughout this book, you've seen how AI supports every stage of your marketing funnel. Let's now visualize your full stack as an integrated system:

Your AI Marketing Engine:

1. **Attract** → Smart ads (Meta, Google, LinkedIn AI)
2. **Capture** → AI-optimized landing pages (Unbounce, Instapage)
3. **Nurture** → Email & content automation (Mailchimp AI, Jasper, Copy.ai)
4. **Convert** → Predictive scoring, chatbots, personalized offers
5. **Retain** → Churn detection, re-engagement workflows
6. **Optimize** → Analytics & decision dashboards (GA4, Looker Studio)

Pro tip: Review and refine this stack quarterly. Even small shifts in tools or timing can unlock major performance gains.

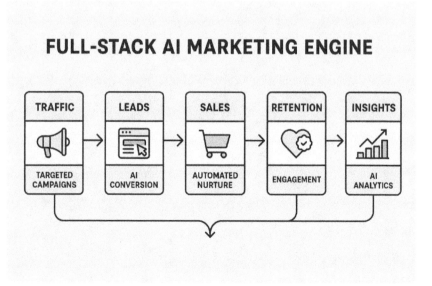

FULL-STACK AI MARKETING ENGINE

TRAFFIC	LEADS	SALES	RETENTION	INSIGHTS
TARGETED CAMPAIGNS	AI CONVERSION	AUTOMATED NURTURE	ENGAGEMENT	AI ANALYTICS

Automating Your Business Backend

While marketing gets the spotlight, the *backend* of your business is where AI can unlock serious efficiency—and sanity.

Automate these operations next:

- **Appointment scheduling:** Tools like Calendly + AI reminders
- **Customer support:** Help desk AI (e.g., HelpScout, Intercom)
- **Bookkeeping & invoices:** QuickBooks + Dext (AI expense categorization)
- **Internal reporting:** Zapier/Make + AI dashboards
- **Hiring & onboarding:** AI resume screening (e.g., Breezy HR)

Rule of thumb: If it's repetitive and rule-based, it can probably be automated.

Bonus gain: Backend automation frees up *mental bandwidth* so you can stay in strategic mode—not stuck in ops.

When to Outsource vs. When to Automate

Not everything should be handed to a tool—or outsourced blindly. The smartest SMBs use a hybrid model: automate where precision wins, outsource where judgment matters.

Outsource when:

- You need deep creative or strategy
- Human empathy is essential (e.g., high-touch sales, sensitive support)
- Brand voice or messaging is complex

Automate when:

- The task is data-driven or repeatable
- Response time matters more than nuance
- You want scalability without more staff

Decision matrix:

Task	Automate or Outsource?
Lead follow-up emails	Automate
Weekly blog strategy	Outsource
Email performance reports	Automate
Customer onboarding calls	Outsource
Ad creative variations	Automate + Review

AUTOMATE VS. OUTSOURCE

	AUTOMATE	CREATIVE & SPECIALIZED
REPETITIVE	INVOICING EMAIL MARKETING SOCIAL POSTING	
OUTSOURCE	CUSTOMER SUPPORT LEAD OUTREACH PAYROLL	SEO WRITING GRAPHIC DESIGN IT SERVICES

How to Grow Without Growing Overhead

AI helps SMBs scale without bloated teams or budgets. Here's how to grow lean and strong:

Lean growth tactics:

- Use no-code tools to build internal systems
- Repurpose content with AI to 10x your visibility
- Score leads automatically and focus only on high-value outreach
- Set retention workflows to run 24/7
- Automate customer feedback and survey analysis

Monthly growth habits:

- Review your marketing funnel KPIs
- Audit tool usage—cut what's not performing
- Run a new A/B test each month
- Spend 2 hours/month trying one new AI feature

Smart move: Build internal SOPs that include your AI stack—so your team knows how to scale *with* the tools.

The 5-Year SMB AI Roadmap

You don't need to do everything at once. Here's how a small business can evolve its AI maturity over time:

Year 1: Foundations

- Adopt 2–3 AI tools for content, email, and simple automations
- Build a basic funnel with landing page + nurture sequence
- Set up dashboards with alerts

Year 2: Integration

- Connect tools across departments (sales, support, ops)
- Use predictive analytics to forecast and plan
- Automate backend functions (invoicing, scheduling, hiring)

Year 3: Optimization

- Start segmenting and personalizing every touchpoint
- Introduce advanced testing (subject lines, creative variants)
- Train staff on prompt engineering and ethical AI use

Year 4–5: Intelligence-First Marketing

- Use AI to recommend product/service strategy
- AI suggests budget allocation across campaigns
- Real-time funnel optimization becomes standard

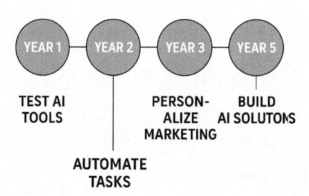

AI ROADMAP FOR SMALL BUSINESS

YEAR 1 — YEAR 2 — YEAR 3 — YEAR 5

TEST AI TOOLS

AUTOMATE TASKS

PERSON-ALIZE MARKETING

BUILD AI SOLUTONS

Conclusion

You don't need to "become an AI company" to win—you just need to *work smarter*. The businesses that build adaptable, intelligent systems now will own the next decade. Your AI marketing engine isn't about replacing your team—it's about *empowering* them. Let AI do the heavy lifting so your people can do what they do best: create, connect, and grow.

Next Steps:
You've got the engine. But before you hit the gas, make sure you're not dragging any bad habits behind. Our final bonus chapter dives into the most common AI mistakes—and how to fix them before they cost you time, money, or trust.

BONUS Chapter: AI Mistakes to Avoid (and How to Fix Them)

Introduction

AI can make your business faster, smarter, and leaner—but only *if* it's used wisely. While success stories are everywhere, so are the horror stories: automated emails gone rogue, chatbots losing leads, and analytics dashboards that tell you everything *except* what to do.

This bonus chapter is your safety net. It's not about fear—it's about *awareness*. We'll break down the most common AI mistakes small and midsize businesses make when adopting new tech, and more importantly, show you exactly how to avoid them. If you read only one chapter twice, let it be this one.

Mistake #1: Letting the Tools Drive the Strategy

The Pitfall:
You find a shiny new AI tool, fall in love with its features, and start reorganizing your marketing around it. Before you know it, you're reacting to tool limitations instead of driving your goals forward.

Real-World Example:
An SMB owner builds their email strategy around a limited automation tool—then can't scale or segment as needed, but is too deep in to switch.

The Fix:
- ✅ Start with your *outcome*, not your app
- ✅ Ask: "What's the problem I'm solving?" not "What's the tool I'm buying?"
- ✅ Build processes first, then choose tech to support them

Pro Tip: Treat AI like an employee. Would you hire someone just because they're "cool" or "fast," or because they fill a gap in your business?

Mistake #2: Automating Before Understanding

The Pitfall:
You automate a workflow you haven't truly mapped. Result? Leads fall through cracks, errors compound, and you're debugging a machine you never fully understood.

Real-World Example:
A retailer automates abandoned cart emails—but forgets to test discount logic. Customers get the wrong offers, damaging trust and revenue.

The Fix:

☑ Manually run your workflow once—then automate

☑ Diagram every input, trigger, and condition first

☑ Always run sandbox tests with dummy data before going live

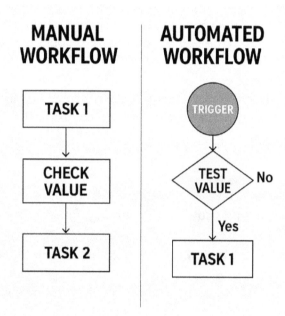

Mistake #3: Relying on AI Content Without Human Editing

The Pitfall:
You paste AI-generated blogs, emails, or social posts straight into your marketing channels. Fast? Yes. Effective? Rarely.

Real-World Example:
A service business posts AI-written blogs weekly, but bounce rates skyrocket. Why? The tone feels robotic, the tips are generic, and nothing sounds *like them*.

The Fix:

☑ Use AI for drafts, not delivery

☑ Build brand voice guides with examples to feed your AI

☑ Edit with intention: personalize intros, add examples, include emotion

Quick Win Checklist for Editing AI Content:

- Is it clear?
- Is it on-brand?
- Is it useful or just filler?
- Is there a clear next step or CTA?
- Does it sound like *you*?

RAW AI OUTPUT	FINAL VERSION
Enhance your space with our top-notch cabinets. Crafted from durable materials, they combine function and style to complement kitchens, bathrooms, and more. Get in touch today for more information!	Upgrade your home with our premium cabinets. Built from high-quality materials, they balance functionality with timeless design, perfect for kitchens, bathrooms, and beyond. Contact us today to learn more!

Mistake #4: Measuring Activity, Not Impact

The Pitfall:
You fall in love with dashboards—clicks, opens, visitors—but fail to measure what actually moves your business: leads, revenue, satisfaction, and retention.

Real-World Example:
A company celebrates 10,000 website visits, but only converts 3 customers. The real problem? Slow page speed and vague CTAs—hidden behind the vanity metrics.

The Fix:
☑ Define 2–3 *North Star* metrics: e.g., cost per lead, email-to-sale rate, customer retention
☑ Use AI tools with *actionable* insights, not just pretty charts
☑ Check metrics weekly, not monthly

Better Metrics to Watch:

- Conversion per campaign, not open rate
- Average time to conversion
- Customer lifetime value (CLV)
- Funnel completion rates by segment

Mistake #5: Over-Personalizing to the Point of Creepiness

The Pitfall:
You use every bit of data—browsing, geography, device, even inferred behavior—to create "hyper-personalized" experiences. But instead of feeling helpful, they feel invasive.

Real-World Example:
A shopper browses shoes once and is then flooded with 12 ads, a triggered SMS, and a follow-up email using their name—all before dinner.

The Fix:
- ✅ Follow the golden rule: *Personalize with permission*
- ✅ Use behavioral cues, not personal data, for messaging
- ✅ Provide opt-outs for personalization wherever possible

Ask yourself:
"If I were the customer, would this feel like insight—or surveillance?"

Mistake #6: Thinking "AI = Set and Forget"

The Pitfall:
You launch an AI campaign, see early wins, then leave it running untouched for months. Over time, quality drops, behavior changes, and results flatline—or worse.

Real-World Example:
A lead-gen funnel that converted at 12% now converts at 3%—but no one noticed for 6 weeks because "the AI had it."

The Fix:
☑ Schedule monthly reviews for all AI-driven campaigns
☑ Refresh creative, messaging, and rules quarterly
☑ Monitor "hidden decay" metrics—engagement drop, bounce rate climb, opt-out rate

Good AI is like a garden.
Automated? Yes. Self-sufficient? Never.

Mistake #7: Ignoring the Human Factor

The Pitfall:
You build perfect systems and workflows—but your *team* doesn't know how to use them, trust them, or explain them to customers.

Real-World Example:
Support reps don't understand the chatbot logic, so they confuse users further. Marketing doesn't know how lead scoring works, so they send everyone the same campaign.

The Fix:

- ☑ Document everything (with screenshots and use cases)
- ☑ Train your team quarterly on the AI stack
- ☑ Encourage feedback on where AI helps—or hurts—day-to-day work
- ☑ Create AI champions inside your team to drive adoption

INTERNAL AI ADOPTION

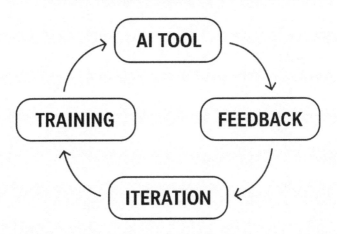

The AI-Ready Recovery Plan: What to Do if You've Already Made Mistakes

Don't worry—everyone has.

If your stack is messy, your team overwhelmed, or your workflows out of sync, here's how to reboot with confidence:

The 7-Day AI Recovery Sprint:

Day 1: Audit all AI tools—what's active, what's used, what's wasted
Day 2: Identify key workflows—content, emails, funnels, ads
Day 3: Interview 2–3 team members about pain points
Day 4: Simplify—eliminate, merge, or pause unnecessary automations
Day 5: Reconnect tools to a shared dashboard
Day 6: Relaunch one small campaign with clean logic
Day 7: Debrief, document, and reset review cycles

Remember:
AI should reduce stress, not cause it. If it's not making your business lighter, faster, and better—it's time to realign.

Conclusion

AI is here to stay—but so are human instincts, creativity, and relationships. Avoiding these common mistakes won't just protect your business—it'll make sure your tech *works for you*, not the other way around.

Use this chapter as a regular check-in. Reread it quarterly. Share it with your team. Because the businesses that win with AI won't be the ones who do the most—they'll be the ones who *do it right*.

CHECK YOUR BONUS AT THE END !

Glossary: AI Marketing Terms Made Simple

AI (Artificial Intelligence)

Software that mimics human learning, decision-making, and creativity using data and pattern recognition. In marketing, AI helps automate tasks, analyze behavior, and create content faster and smarter.

Automation

The process of setting up systems or tools to run tasks on their own, without manual effort—like sending follow-up emails, scheduling social posts, or tagging leads based on behavior.

Behavioral Segmentation

Grouping customers based on actions (e.g., clicks, purchases, email opens) instead of just demographics. Helps deliver more relevant marketing.

Chatbot

An AI-powered assistant that interacts with visitors or customers via chat. Used for answering questions, qualifying leads, or guiding users to the right resource.

Churn Rate

The percentage of customers who stop buying, subscribing, or engaging with your business over time. AI can help detect churn early and trigger re-engagement.

Conversion Rate

The percentage of users who take a desired action—like making a purchase, filling out a form, or booking a demo. A key measure of funnel performance.

Copy.ai / Jasper / ChatGPT

Popular AI writing tools that generate content for blogs, emails, ads, and more. Each one has strengths in tone, workflow, and speed.

Customer Journey / Funnel

The step-by-step path a visitor takes from discovering your brand to becoming a loyal customer. Funnels include stages like attract, capture, nurture, convert, and retain.

Dynamic Content

Website or email content that changes based on user behavior or traits. For example, a headline that updates based on location or past visits.

Exit-Intent Popup

A message or offer triggered when a visitor is about to leave your website. Often used to capture leads or prevent abandonment.

Lead Scoring

Assigning a score to each lead based on how engaged or qualified they are. AI improves this by analyzing patterns in user behavior.

Lookalike Audience

An advertising audience created from your existing customer data. Platforms like Meta and Google use AI to find people who behave like your current buyers.

Marketing Automation

Using software to streamline, schedule, and trigger marketing activities (like email sequences or SMS follow-ups) based on defined rules or behavior.

Meta Advantage+ / Google Performance Max

AI-powered advertising features that handle targeting, bidding, and creative optimization across multiple ad formats for maximum efficiency.

No-Code Tool

A platform that allows you to build workflows, apps, or automations without writing code. Tools like Zapier, Tidio, and Unbounce fall into this category.

North Star Metric

Your primary business growth metric—like leads generated, cost per sale, or recurring revenue. Everything should align with improving this number.

Opt-In / Consent

When a user gives permission for tracking, communication, or personalization. Ethical AI marketing requires clear and informed consent.

Personalization

Tailoring your messaging, offers, or content to the individual user. AI enables this at scale—but it must be done responsibly to avoid feeling invasive.

Predictive Analytics

Using AI to forecast future behavior based on past patterns. Example: predicting who's likely to buy, churn, or engage based on their activity.

Prompt (AI Prompt)

A specific instruction or input you give to an AI tool to get a useful output. For example: "Write a friendly email introducing our spring collection."

Retargeting

Showing ads to users who've already interacted with your brand (e.g., visited your site or added to cart). Often driven by AI for better timing and messaging.

RightMessage / Tidio / HubSpot AI

Popular tools that use AI for personalized user experiences, lead capture, and intelligent automation across your website and CRM.

Smart Dashboard

An analytics display that uses AI to highlight what matters most—like dropping conversions, sudden trends, or customer churn signals.

Triggered Sequence

An automated series of emails, messages, or actions that activate based on a user's action—like signing up for a webinar or viewing your pricing page.

User Experience (UX)

How a customer experiences your site, content, or product. AI-enhanced UX feels fast, relevant, and intuitive—not confusing or invasive.

Vanity Metric

A surface-level stat (like social likes or page views) that doesn't always translate into real business results. AI helps you focus on what *actually* drives revenue.

Zero-Data Personalization

Personalized experiences based on real-time behavior—not stored personal data. A privacy-friendly way to offer relevance without tracking users long-term.

Bonus – FREE eBook Version

Want the full-color PDF version of this book?
Simply email me at **ericl@acrasolution.com** with a **screenshot of your Amazon purchase and positive review**, and I'll gladly send you your personal copy.

Thank you for taking the time to read this eBook.

Your support means more than you know. **By purchasing this book, you're directly contributing to the creation of more high-quality, practical resources** for business owners, IT leaders, and everyday professionals navigating the complex world of cybersecurity. It's because of readers like you that I can continue researching, writing, and delivering tools that make a real difference.

Whether you leave a positive review, recommend this book to a colleague, or simply apply what you've learned — **you're helping grow a stronger, safer business community. And for that, I sincerely thank you.**

At **AcraSolution**, we're committed to providing both premium services and a wide range of **free, actionable tools**. Our growing library includes documentation, articles, and step-by-step guides — designed to bring you immediate value, no strings attached.

If you need additional guidance or support, don't hesitate to visit our website www.acrasolution.com or reach out directly.

Together, we can build a more secure future.

— Eric LeBouthillier
Author & Cybersecurity Strategist